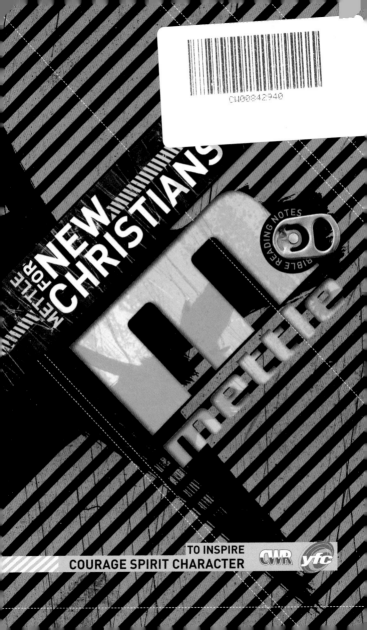

METTLE FOR

NEW
CHRISTIANS

BIBLE READING NOTES

mettle

TO INSPIRE
COURAGE SPIRIT CHARACTER

CWR yfc

Published 2008 by CWR, Waverley Abbey House, Waverley Lane, Farnham,
Surrey GU9 8EP, England. Registered Charity No. 294387. Registered
Limited Company No. 1990308.

Mettle for New Christians is produced in association with British Youth for
Christ. British Youth for Christ is part of Youth for Christ International, a
movement of youth evangelism organisations in over 100 countries of the
world. Please visit www.yfci.org for the country nearest you.

See back of book for list of National Distributors.

Whilst all reasonable effort has been made to source the poem by Petra
Crane, we have been unable to locate the original details of publication.

Concept development by YFC and CWR.
Editing design and production by CWR.
Printed in England by Nuffield Press.

ISBN: 978-1-85345-459-2

CONTENTS

INTRODUCTION

So where do we begin? Well, let's start with you! I don't know how you got this book – whether it was from a friend, or at an event, or you simply picked it up from a coffee table somewhere. To be honest, it doesn't matter. What is important is that you are reading it, and that you realise it is no accident you have this book in your hands! How do I know this? Read on ...

GETTING THE MOST OUT OF METTLE

What type of person are you? Here is a short quiz to find out how you can best read this book to get the most out of it.

1. When the TV programme you're watching has a commercial break, you:
   a) Channel hop to see what else is on.
   b) Keep watching. You don't want to miss the next part of the programme!
   c) Leave the room to make a drink/get a snack, hoping that you'll get back in time.

2. A band you like is due to release a new album. You:
   a) Think, 'Great! I'll have to get that.'
   b) Pre-order your copy.
   c) Go online on its release date and download it.

3. You are after some new trainers and decide to take a look at eBay. They have loads you like, so you:
   a) Click to 'watch item' on several pairs.
   b) Find a 'buy it now' pair to make sure you get them.
   c) Make some bids and monitor what happens.

4. Assuming you are alone and you like them ...
you open a pot of Pringles, and:
a) Find that 'once you pop you can't stop'.
b) Measure out what you want and keep some
for later.
c) Eat as much as you want.

5. You have a piece of work due in. You:
a) Leave it until nearer the deadline: 'Life's busy!'
b) Do it now: 'Best out of the way!'
c) Think about what needs to be done and plan
it out over the time available.

YOUR BEST READ

Remember, this is meant to be a fun quiz that
gets you thinking about how you can best read
this book. If you don't think the answer you get
fits you, choose an alternative challenge that fits
you and sign up! It's good to commit.

NOW TURN OVERLEAF TO FIND
THE YOUR BEST FIT ▶▶

You like to see what's on offer and make your choices accordingly. Sometimes you miss out or pass deadlines but think life's too short to worry. You will probably scan through this book looking for bits that catch your eye and quickly decide whether it will be kept on a bookshelf (good to have around but not used much) or in the toilet (good to pick up when you have a moment).

YOUR CHALLENGE

Count to ten and make yourself read it a week at a time (week one, two etc). You are only committing yourself to a week of daily readings! And I will guarantee that within that week's worth of reading, there will be something that will help you in years to come.

Sign up and take the challenge:

Sign: .... Date: ....

You like to be prepared and know what is going to happen next. You get frustrated with others and their lack of commitment, as you try to not let anyone down. You will probably read this book cover to cover – someone thought it was important enough to give to you, so it must contain some valuable stuff.

YOUR CHALLENGE

As you go through the book, stop and make notes. Give yourself time to think about what you're reading, and take time out to ask about what something means if you disagree. Talk about what you have read with other Christians. Sometimes you have to squeeze something to get the most out of it!

Sign up and take the challenge:

Sign: _____ Date: _____

Mostly Cs

You like to go with the flow but you want to be in control. You like to connect the things you do and happen to you, then share that knowledge with others: 'That reminds me ... I read something about that!' You will probably read this book one stage at a time, day by day, but may stumble on remembering to make a regular time.

YOUR CHALLENGE

Commit to a time slot – early morning before you get up, last thing before you go to sleep, or anything in between, whatever suits you. Be willing to adjust the timings if you need to. You are in control and will get the best out of this book by making and committing to the time.

Sign up and take the challenge:

Sign: _____ Date: _____

me

SECTION 01//ME

KEY VERSE
v17

'This means that anyone who belongs to Christ has become a new person. The old life is gone; a new life has begun!'

HAVE YOU EVER WANTED TO START OVER?

It's easy with a computer game. You just press restart and there you are, back at the beginning again. But is life really like that? Is there a restart button?

Reread today's verses. You are a new person.

DAY 01

10

In all the world there is nobody like you.
Since the beginning of time, there has never been
    another person like you,
Nobody has your smile, your eyes, your hands,
    your hair.
Nobody owns your handwriting, your voice.
You're special.
Nobody can paint your brush strokes.
Nobody has your taste for food or music or dance
    or art.
Nobody in the universe sees things as you do.
In all time there has never been anybody who
    laughs in exactly your way.
And what makes you laugh or cry or think
May cause a totally different response in another,
So ... you're special.[1]

When you become a Christian, you have the opportunity to start living in the fullness that God has for your unique life. The poem and the Bible verses are true! The old life has gone and a new life has begun. You are brought back, through Jesus, to be the person God created you to be. Remember: 'Since the beginning of time, there has never been another person like you.'

WHAT'S IT TO ME?

We cannot restart our lives at the push of a button. But we can, through Jesus, get rid of the negative and bad things that hold us back. The hurt may remain but Jesus understands and is around to help.

We will continue to look at the poem opposite over the next two days, so that we can draw out the different points of the unique person who is you.

PRAY

Father, help me to know I am special – as who I am, as who You made me to be. Help me not to try to be anyone else, but to enjoy things and laugh in my own way. Thank You for creating me. Amen.

1. Poem by Petra Crane, origin unknown.

'But our bodies have many parts, and God has put each part just where he wants it.'

DAY 02

12

You are different from any other person who has
  ever lived in all history.
You are the only one in the whole of creation
Who has your particular set of abilities.
There is always someone who is better at one thing
  or another than you,
But no one has your combination of talents and
  feelings.
Through all eternity, no one will ever walk, talk,
  think
Or do anything exactly like you.
You're special.[1]

WE ARE ALL DIFFERENT! In 1 Corinthians 12, the apostle Paul explains the importance of realis-ing this. If we were all the same, how would we get anything done? Paul uses the example of the human body to show that there are many parts of the Church. No part of the body is more important than another – each has its own different and unique job to do.

WHAT'S IT TO ME?

We sometimes struggle to get the balance between being unique and fitting in with those around us. And what might seem the right thing for us to do one day could feel completely wrong the next day! Life is always changing, developing, growing. Today's reading should encourage and challenge you. You are important, and God wants to be a part of your life. He wants to get involved and be with you. He wants to help you to know Him better and to know the good plans He has for your life. But you make the choice to include Him in your life each day ... or not.

THINK

God has placed us where we are. He knows us and what makes us walk, talk and think. He knows how we will react to things. He knows exactly where we fit.

1. Poem by Petra Crane, origin unknown.

KEY VERSE
v10

'... so we can do the good things he planned for us long ago.'

You're rare, and in all rarity there is enormous value
And because of your great value,
The need for you to imitate anyone else is absolutely unnecessary.
You're special ... and it's no accident you are.
Please realise God has made you for a special purpose.
He has a job for you to do as well as you can.
Out of the billions of applicants, only one is qualified.
Only one has the unique and right combination of what it takes,
And that one is you.[1]

WE HAVE BEEN SAVED FOR A PURPOSE, FOR 'GOOD THINGS [GOD] PLANNED FOR US LONG AGO' (V.10).

This poem ends with the idea that only you have the 'unique and right combination of what it takes' to do the job God has prepared for you.

WHAT'S IT TO ME?

So, how do you feel? Are you ready to accept that God created the unique you, that you are made in a certain way, for a special purpose? There is more to life than lots of people think. It's not 'You live, you die, game over'. There is a reason for our being here. But it doesn't always look like that, does it?

As we continue through the following days, we will be looking at creation, what went wrong and why the world is as it is. And we will be looking at the solution to all our lives: Jesus! We'll be discovering more about Him and finding out about how we can apply that understanding to our lives.

PRAY

Father in heaven, thank You for valuing me just as I am! Help me to feel comfortable with who You made me to be. And help me to feel confident that in Your power I can do the job You have made me to do. Amen.

'... God looked over all he had made, and he saw that it was very good!'

KEY VERSE v31

DAY 04

16

HAVE YOU EVER WONDERED WHAT YOU WERE CREATED FOR?

HAVE YOU EVER THOUGHT ABOUT HOW YOU GOT HERE?

HAVE YOU EVER ASKED WHY YOU ARE ALIVE?

HAVE YOU EVER HAD ANY ACCEPTABLE ANSWERS?

This is the very beginning. The Bible goes through the whole creation process, from an empty darkness, to God resting after He had finished making everything. (Even evolutionists agree the world developed in the same order as detailed in the Bible!)

In the reading today, God is looking at what He has created: '... he saw that it was very good' – in every way. He loved it! He thought it was great. He was pleased with what He had done.

Have you ever looked up at the sky on a clear night? You are actually seeing millions of miles! The stars and moon, even a planet on occasions ... How insignificant are we?! Yet look at all we do; we really are at the top of the scale – we invent, we cure, we communicate globally.

WHAT'S IT TO ME?

God put humans in charge of everything He created 'putting all things under [our] authority' (see Psa. 8:6). But what are we doing with the power God has entrusted to us? How are we going about dealing with our responsibility to God, each other, and the planet?

Originally, when God made the world, it was good. Something happened, though, and we don't always see that good, we see trouble and sadness. We'll look at this tomorrow. But remember, God designed you for a specific purpose. He loves and accepts you just as you are, and will give you the power to fulfil the plans He has for you.

THINK

Try to ignore those 'bad hair days' or lack of sporting ability. God looks past everything you are feeling, and sees how He made you. He loves you completely. Talk to God about how you feel about yourself. Ask Him to show you how He feels about you.

'The woman was convinced ... [the] fruit looked delicious, and she wanted the wisdom it would give her.'

KEY VERSE v6

DAY 05

18

SO WHAT WENT WRONG? Everything was perfect in the Garden of Eden, until the serpent had a chat with Eve, who then had a chat with Adam: 'Yum! It looks good, it smells good, so it must be good! Who says we can't try it? Why not? It can't hurt, can it?'

And that's how sin entered the world (sometimes known as the Fall), and it got all messed up.

'Sin' is not a popular word today. It means wrongdoing – hurting God, others and ourselves.

God gave Adam and Eve complete freedom and only asked one thing: 'Don't eat from that tree' (see Gen. 2:16–17). But that is what they did. And how did God react when they disobeyed Him? He got really angry! Read verses 14–24. What happened to the serpent, to Eve and to Adam?

When God asked for an explanation, the response was, 'The serpent deceived me ... That's why I ate it' (v.13). Is that *our* response when we're caught doing something we know is wrong? 'I was tricked, it's somebody else's fault ... they said it would be OK!'

This completely changed Adam and Eve's relationship with their Creator. God had provided for their every need but they chose independence and ruined that relationship. It moved them away from God, to a place of need.

WHAT'S IT TO ME?

As new Christians, there are times when we will be tempted, asking ourselves, 'Did God really say...?' But we're not alone! Others have experienced similar temptations and not given in – and God is always there to help us through. He will keep the temptation from becoming too strong for us to cope with. Read 1 Corinthians 10:13.

CHALLENGE

We need to take responsibility for our actions and think before we act. We are all tempted, but what makes a difference is how we handle it ... and who we turn to for help!

'... the Lord was sorry he had ever made them ... It broke his heart.'

DAY 06

20

SO ADAM AND EVE WERE KICKED OUT OF THE GARDEN OF EDEN AND HUGE ANGELS WITH FLAMING SWORDS WERE STATIONED AROUND THE PLACE TO KEEP THEM OUT. Things got worse (see Gen. 4–5). God was not at all happy with what He saw: 'It broke his heart.'

What did God do? Did He give up on humanity altogether? No. He chose to forgive – and get involved.

God is the loving Creator who saw the world as good, but the serpent (the devil in disguise), with Adam and Eve, spoiled that picture. God is also the Judge of humankind. He judged the world because humanity turned against Him. But He still loved us, so He did an amazing thing. In Romans 5:8 we read: '... God showed his great love for us by sending Christ to die for us while we were still sinners.' So God judged the world because He had to, but He loved us so much that He sent His Son Jesus to save us. Through His death, we were made right in God's sight. How? By dying and then beating death, Jesus reconnected us to God so we can be His friends again. This was not a simple thing to achieve. It meant Jesus taking the blame for all our wrongdoing.

WHAT'S IT TO ME?

Nothing can separate us from the love of God. No fears, worries or even the power of hell (see Rom. 8:38). But what does that really mean to us? For me, it's this: Whatever is happening in my life, God is always there at my side. I can worry and stress about things, even ignore the fact that God is with me, but it makes no difference. He is there, ready and willing to listen, comfort and get involved.

PRAY

Thank You, Jesus, for dying for me to forgive me for all I have done wrong. Help me to understand that You are always around and are interested in me; You want to be involved in what I do and in what I say. Challenge me to make a difference in my daily life. Amen.

JESUS: WHO WAS HE AND WHAT DID HE DO?

We will be finding out what He said about Himself, what others said about Him ... And be challenged to consider what we think about Him.

JESUS

SECTION 02//JESUS

'... to all who believed him and accepted him, he gave the right to become children of God.'

'JESUS CHRIST? WHY HERE, WHY NOW? WHO IS HE, AND WHAT IS HE TO ME?'

Jesus was born onto this earth and Roman historians such as Tacitus and Suetonius wrote about Him. He was a historical figure and fully human, but we are missing out if we leave it there. He fulfilled over 300 Old Testament prophecies about what He was going to do. These things were written hundreds of years before He was born! For example, the prophecy in Micah about His place of birth was fulfilled: 'But you, O Bethlehem Ephrathah, are only a small village ... (in) Judah. Yet a ruler of Israel will come from you, one whose origins are from the distant past' (Micah 5:2). Even the price of Jesus' betrayal by Judas was foretold: 'So they counted out for my wages thirty pieces of silver' (Zech. 11:12). Look up Matthew 26:14–16 to read about this coming true.

Jesus made some claims of His own, too, and others were killed for believing in Him. So why do we hear the name 'Jesus Christ' often used as a swear word (which is a statement of disbelief), and then are asked why we should get offended at such a misuse of His name?

WHAT'S IT TO ME?

Over the coming days we will be looking at Jesus – what claims He made and what other people have said about Him. Let's face it, you need to know what you think and why, so that you can answer the questions 'Who is He and what is He to me?' for yourself.

07 CHALLENGE

You have 'believed him and accepted him'. Because of that, you have become a child of God. Do you really understand what that means? Stop and think about why you became a Christian. Take time to consider what questions you have and note them down. Over the next few weeks, we hope to help you answer some of those questions. Remember, you are not alone. Find a Christian leader or friend to talk to.

'... our Lord Jesus Christ has made us friends of God.'

DAY 08

26

IN HIS BOOK, *QUESTIONS OF LIFE*,[1] NICKY GUMBEL USES AN ILLUSTRATION ABOUT TWO PEOPLE WHO WENT THROUGH SCHOOL AND UNIVERSITY TOGETHER AND FORMED A GREAT FRIENDSHIP. LIFE WENT ON, THEY WENT THEIR DIFFERENT WAYS AND LOST CONTACT. ONE BECAME A JUDGE AND THE OTHER A CRIMINAL.

One day the criminal appeared before the judge. He had committed a crime to which he pleaded guilty. The judge recognised his old friend, and faced a dilemma. He was a judge so he had to be just; he couldn't let the man off. On the other hand, he didn't want to punish the man, because he loved him. So he told his friend that he would fine him the correct penalty for the offence.

But the judge decided to pay the fine for his friend. The judge showed real justice – the penalty had to be paid. But he also showed real love for his old friend when he offered to pay the fine for him.

WHAT'S IT TO ME?

Do you see your life as criminal? Do you understand that humankind has done wrong and we have to be judged against what God says is right? Do you see that Jesus was God's penalty payment, so we could return to what God originally intended for us? If you don't quite understand, ask a trusted Christian friend or leader to explain it to you.

PRAY

Father, thank You for showing Your love for me by sending Jesus. Jesus, thank You for paying the penalty of my sin, and thank You that You died paying that penalty for me. Help me to know You more each day, and to really accept Your friendship. Amen.

---

1. Nicky Gumbel, *Questions of Life* (Eastbourne: Kingsway Publications, 2003).

KEY VERSE
V35

'I am the bread of life.'

DAY 09

28

I REALLY LIKE FRIED BREAKFASTS, CHOCOLATE AND RED GRAPES (NOT ALL ON THE SAME PLATE!). BUT TO FIND OUT IF I LIKED THEM, FIRST I CHOSE TO TRY THEM. WHEN WAS THE LAST TIME YOU TRIED SOMETHING NEW?

Jesus claims that He is the bread of life, and in the verses today, He is speaking to a group of guys about being fed and doing miracles. They had seen Him feed 5,000 people and they wanted to see more, but Jesus saw their real need. They needed to be fed with something that wouldn't go off or that would only satisfy them for a short time. They needed to choose Jesus.

You might look and look but until you try Him, you will never know what Jesus is really like. Choose to build a friendship with Jesus! Each day, spend time reading the Bible and these notes, and talking to others about Him. To get a good overview of Jesus' life, try reading the Gospels (the first few books in the New Testament), possibly starting with Luke. Remember that your relationship with God will take time, so make sure you give it plenty!

WHAT'S IT TO ME?

You may have decided to follow Jesus, but do you know why you are following Him? Have you thought about what committing your life to following Jesus really means? Do you realise the enormity of that choice, and what that means you have to admit to? Think about these questions. Over the next few days, we will find out more about Jesus, and what really following Him will mean for our own lives.

PRAY

Father, help me to be willing to find out more about Jesus and to try new things to understand more of Your love. Amen.

KEY VERSE
v12

'I am the light of the world.'

EVER BEEN BLINDED BY A LIGHT SHINING IN THE DARKNESS? Maybe you've been camping, driving, or posing for a photo and WHAM! If you close your eyes, it's still there, sparkling in the darkness. A bright light shows things up and leaves an impression.

In the passage before our key verse today, Jesus defused an angry mob who were about to kill a woman, saying 'let the one who has never sinned throw the first stone!' (v.7). One by one they left, until Jesus and the woman were alone. 'Didn't even one of them condemn you?' He asked. 'No,' she responded. Jesus replied, 'Neither do I. Go and sin no more' (vv.10–11).

Everyone has a God-given conscience that can be triggered by His Spirit. We saw that happening in the story about the angry crowd. The people thought that they were doing the right thing by bringing this woman to justice, but Jesus challenged them to look at their own lives. Jesus brings about change in people's lives if they allow Him to. When the crowd and the woman left that day, we can be sure they had been challenged and changed; they were *different*, because they had met Him.

WHAT'S IT TO ME?

Jesus sets us an example of how to live. We should look at our own lives and let Jesus shine in to show up the dark bits. Only then, when we admit the darkness is there, can we do something about it.

⊙ CHALLENGE

What's going on in your life? Are you willing for Jesus to shine a light on all aspects of the way you live? What do you need to stop doing in order to start living the way Jesus intends you to live? Do you even know what that looks like? As a start – follow the light: follow Jesus' example.

'I am the gate for the sheep.'

DAY 11

32

'QUICK! LEG IT. HE'S COMING.'
'HURRY UP OR HE'LL CATCH US.'
'IT MUST BE AROUND HERE SOMEWHERE!'
'THERE IT IS. OPEN IT AND LET'S GET OUT
OF HERE.'
'AHHHHH, THE HANDLE HAS COME OFF IN
MY HAND!'
'WHAT?!'

A memory from my past – whilst in someone
else's orchard, 'scrumping' (taking apples).
(By the way, this was a long time ago before I
became a Christian. I wouldn't be doing this
now!) A few mates and I would climb the orchard
wall. Then one would stay as lookout while
the others would go around grabbing as many
apples as possible. If you were lucky, you would
load up and be on your way. If you were unlucky,
the owner would come out and give chase – as
he did on this occasion.

I can still remember the joy of finding the gate
to the orchard ... then the sheer pain and panic of
not being able to get through it.

WHAT'S IT TO ME?

I was trapped and could not escape the situation I was in. My freedom lay on the other side of that gate. In the same way, Jesus offers us an escape route: in the reading today, He is talking about being the way through – 'I am the gate'. He is offering us freedom through a relationship with Him.

It is only when you feel trapped that you realise how important a gate is. Only through Him are we truly free!

PRAY

What are you looking to escape from? Ask Jesus to help. Spend time quietly thinking about all the things that are going on in your life – what is worrying you or getting you down. Then ask for help. Go into detail, talk about how you feel. Be honest, and be open. Jesus will help you find the way through.

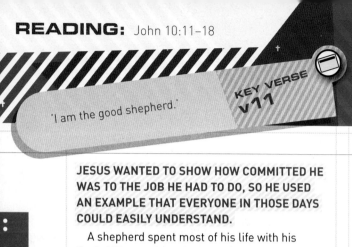

KEY VERSE
v11

'I am the good shepherd.'

DAY 12

34

JESUS WANTED TO SHOW HOW COMMITTED HE WAS TO THE JOB HE HAD TO DO, SO HE USED AN EXAMPLE THAT EVERYONE IN THOSE DAYS COULD EASILY UNDERSTAND.

A shepherd spent most of his life with his flock. His own sheep knew and responded to his voice. He led (not drove) them to fresh grazing, and guarded them from wild animals. Jesus wanted to show the close personal relationship between Himself and each of His followers. He wanted to show the absolute security we have in Him, in His leadership and guidance, in His constant company, in His unfailing care and in His sacrificial love.

Jesus wants you to get to know Him and be able to recognise His voice. When your best friend telephones, you don't need to ask who it is. You recognise their voice when they say 'Hello'. Just as it took time to get to know your best friend, it takes time to get to know Jesus. You can build your relationship through reading the Bible, by talking to others about God and by spending time talking to God through prayer.

WHAT'S IT TO ME?

Get to know Jesus. Did you realise that you can experience this level of relationship with Jesus? He wants to get to know you and has proved that He is open to this level of relationship – are you?

CHALLENGE

To be able to trust Jesus and have this kind of relationship with Him, you need to spend time with Him. You've already started this by using these notes, so if you have a big decision to make, try asking Him for some guidance. Make sure you give Him a chance, and space, to answer! Sit quietly and allow time to hear His voice. Remember that He will not contradict what He has said in the Bible, so if you are in doubt about what God is saying to you, talk to a trusted Christian leader and ask for clarification.

KEY VERSE
v6

'I am the way, the truth, and the life.'

DAY 13

36

**HERE JESUS IS EXPLAINING TO HIS DISCIPLES
WHAT IS ABOUT TO HAPPEN IN HIS LIFE, AND
THEIRS.** They have just been told that one of
them is going to betray Jesus, and that Peter is
going to deny Him three times. Sure, there have
been ups and downs working and living with
Jesus, but He has always been around to sort
things out. Now He is telling them that He is
going to die: He is going to leave them! They are
worried and confused.

Jesus sees this and explains that He has to die
so that He can return to the Father, so making the
approach road for them (and us) to come to God.
We've already seen that it is through our belief
in Jesus that we can be received and accepted by
God the Father.

Jesus goes on to talk about how God is sending a counsellor and encourager, the Holy Spirit,
who will never leave us and will lead us in truth
throughout our lives (vv.15–26). Jesus is revealing
God's plan to us, the three-in-one God: God the

Creator, who made the universe and everything in it; Jesus, the Interceder, who through His death came to bring us back to a relationship with God; and the Holy Spirit, the Helper, who shows us how to live every day.

WHAT'S IT TO ME?

Each 'part' of God is important and we need to understand what part each 'Person' plays. We recognise that God created us to be in relationship with Him but through Adam and Eve things went wrong and that relationship was broken. God sent Jesus to make right our relationship and make a way through back to God. Jesus sent the Holy Spirit to help His disciples ' ... he will teach you everything and will remind you of everything I [Jesus] have told you' (v.26).

THINK

If you know Jesus, you know God, and you can also know the Holy Spirit. Ask the Holy Spirit to guide, advise and encourage you. Remember, He will never leave you.

'Then he asked them,
" ... who do you say I am?"'

WE HAVE LOOKED AT SOME OF THE CLAIMS JESUS
MADE ABOUT HIMSELF. IN THE FOLLOWING
NOTES, WE ARE GOING TO EXPLORE SOME OF THE
RESPONSES TO HIS CLAIMS. HOW DID PEOPLE
ANSWER HIS QUESTION: 'WHO DO YOU SAY I AM?'?

MY STORY AND MY RESPONSE

At fourteen, I was challenged to respond to this
question myself. I had to think through what my
response would be. It was early spring when the
grass starts to be cut, when the trees start to
blossom, and the River Walk near where I lived
starts to show life ... fresh smells, vivid colours
and the wonder of newly-hatched ducklings.
Walking home through the River Walk, I was
struck by the wonder of all that was around me. If
all this was truly made by God, and through Jesus
I could have a relationship with God the Creator,
what was I waiting for? So my response to this
question was: 'I believe Jesus is the Son of God.'

WHAT'S IT TO ME?

Things didn't all suddenly fall into place in my life. What did happen was that I started a friendship with God that I now rely on completely. In every situation, I know God is there encouraging, challenging and helping me. As with any new relationship, it took time to build. Through reading the Bible, looking at what Jesus did and talking about it to others, my understanding of the friendship grew and is still growing now.

THINK

The famous author C.S. Lewis (who wrote The Chronicles of Narnia amongst other things) summed it up like this: we have three options about who we think Jesus is. One: He's who He said He is. Two: He was a complete lunatic. Three: He was something much worse! But C.S. Lewis then went on to conclude that his understanding and experience of Jesus led him to only one conclusion: Jesus was, and is, God.

Jesus is asking you, 'Who do you say I am?' What is your story? What is your response?

'You are the Messiah, the Son of the living God.'

KEY VERSE
v16

DAY 15

40

PETER, FROM GALILEE, WAS A FISHERMAN WHEN JESUS ASKED HIM TO BECOME ONE OF HIS DISCIPLES. A COUPLE OF YEARS LATER, PETER MADE THE STATEMENT WE SEE IN OUR DISPLAYED VERSE TODAY: 'YOU ARE THE MESSIAH, THE SON OF THE LIVING GOD.'

Peter had been through a lot in the years he had been with Jesus. He'd heard Jesus teach, he'd seen Jesus heal people, he'd helped Jesus feed 5,000 people and he had even walked on water!

Peter first answered a call to follow Jesus, and only then was he able to be part of these things. Peter's story was a journey. He didn't always have all the answers; he had doubts and he got scared. When things got hard for the disciples, Jesus even asked Peter if he wanted to leave and stop following Him, but Peter's response was 'Lord, to whom would we go? You have the words that give eternal life. We believe, and we know you are the Holy One of God' (see John 6:68–69).

WHAT'S IT TO ME?

Our understanding of Jesus takes time to develop; it is through our experience and knowledge of Jesus that we really get to know Him. And every so often, we have to stop and be challenged, like Peter was by Jesus, about what we think and how this affects our life. It is OK to have doubts and struggles and to fail, but we need to take everything to Jesus and ask Him for help. Only He has the words of eternal life.

THINK

In all relationships, we can think back to some great memories. Can you remember any times when God was involved in your life, even before you may have made a decision to believe in Him? Do you want to have some memories like Peter's? If you have answered the call to follow Jesus, you can!

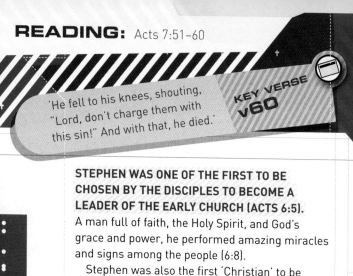

KEY VERSE
v60

'He fell to his knees, shouting, "Lord, don't charge them with this sin!" And with that, he died.'

DAY 16

42

STEPHEN WAS ONE OF THE FIRST TO BE CHOSEN BY THE DISCIPLES TO BECOME A LEADER OF THE EARLY CHURCH (ACTS 6:5). A man full of faith, the Holy Spirit, and God's grace and power, he performed amazing miracles and signs among the people (6:8).

Stephen was also the first 'Christian' to be killed for his belief and defence of God. In Acts 7:51–60 we find him defending himself in front of the Sanhedrin (Jewish council of leaders) against the charge of blasphemy. Stephen showed no fear; he stood up for what he believed, he told the truth and he even asked God to forgive those who were stoning him to death!

Stephen was utterly convinced that Jesus was the Son of God. He was so convinced that he was willing to die for saying so.

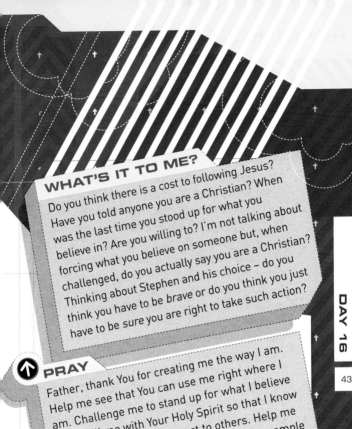

WHAT'S IT TO ME?

Do you think there is a cost to following Jesus? Have you told anyone you are a Christian? When was the last time you stood up for what you believe in? Are you willing to? I'm not talking about forcing what you believe on someone but, when challenged, do you actually say you are a Christian? Thinking about Stephen and his choice – do you think you have to be brave or do you think you just have to be sure you are right to take such action?

PRAY

Father, thank You for creating me the way I am. Help me see that You can use me right where I am. Challenge me to stand up for what I believe in and fill me with Your Holy Spirit so that I know what to say and how to react to others. Help me to be mindful of my friends and to be an example to them as I live each day for You, no matter what situations I find myself in. Amen.

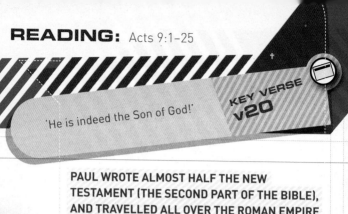

KEY VERSE
V20

'He is indeed the Son of God!'

DAY 17

44

PAUL WROTE ALMOST HALF THE NEW TESTAMENT (THE SECOND PART OF THE BIBLE), AND TRAVELLED ALL OVER THE ROMAN EMPIRE TELLING PEOPLE ABOUT JESUS. But when we first meet Paul, at the stoning to death of Stephen, he is called Saul. He is out to get the Christians, as he believes they are wrong about their belief in Jesus. He takes every opportunity to throw them into prison and to stir trouble up against them: '... Saul was uttering threats with every breath and was eager to kill the Lord's followers' (v.1). He was a man on a mission!

Here we find him travelling to Damascus, when he is hit by a brilliant beam of light. He is blinded and has a conversation with Jesus. Then, in Damascus, Ananias, a believer, is sent by God to pray for Saul to regain his sight and to receive the Holy Spirit. Faithfully, Ananias did this and Saul went on to be baptised and to boldly preach that Jesus was indeed the Son of God.

Saul (later, 'Paul') was convinced that Jesus was the Son of God. He powerfully spoke to others; so much so that the Jewish leaders decided to have him murdered.

WHAT'S IT TO ME?

Over the last three days we have read about people who were willing to change and risk their lives for believing in Jesus. How have you changed through your experience and knowledge of Jesus? How bold or faithful do you feel? Remember, the power to live for Jesus comes through the Holy Spirit living in us.

PRAY

Father, thank You for giving us such examples of faith. Thank You that Ananias faithfully went to see Saul and prayed for him, even though he was worried about what response he would get. Challenge me to stand up for what I believe, and give me the strength to do what You ask, through Your Holy Spirit. Amen.

'Once Jesus was ... praying. As he finished, one of his disciples ... said, "Lord, teach us to pray, just as John taught his disciples."'

HOW DO WE PRAY? WHAT SHOULD WE PRAY? SOMETIMES WE JUST DON'T KNOW WHERE TO START.

Jesus gave us what has become called the Lord's Prayer as a model for our own personal prayers. Simply put, this prayer outlines all we basically need to ask God for. It says we must approach God as our Father, asking that His will be done and not ours. It tells us to ask God for the things we need in this life and for forgiveness for the wrong things we've done and have had done to us.

It's the most important prayer we can use as Christians. As we pray through the different stages, it inspires other, more specific things we need to pray for. We all have different prayers and different needs, yet the basic truth remains: we pray for God's kingdom to come on the earth, we must be a forgiving people, and we should rely on God for all that we need in life. Our prayer requests are just that: *requests*. Our requests may be met with a Yes, a No or a Not Yet, but we will never be let down by God. He will always give us what we need.

WHAT'S IT TO ME?

Through Jesus, we are able to talk to God. And, in the reading today, Jesus teaches us a simple way of doing just that. If we follow Jesus' instructions, we will be able to deepen and strengthen our relationship with God.

CHALLENGE

Take each line of the Lord's Prayer and read it aloud. Pause, think and pray your own personal prayers that fit in with each of Jesus' instructions. Perhaps there's someone you need to forgive? Perhaps you need to focus more on God being your heavenly Father? (You might find that difficult, depending on your relationship with your earthly dad. Remember, God is a perfect Father. Ask someone you trust to pray and help you find God as your Father.)

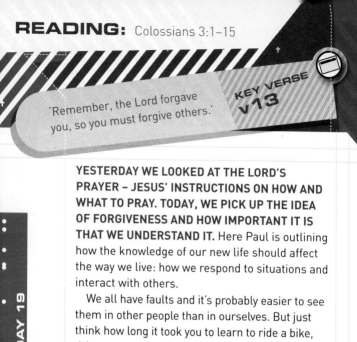

KEY VERSE
v13

'Remember, the Lord forgave you, so you must forgive others.'

DAY 19

48

YESTERDAY WE LOOKED AT THE LORD'S PRAYER – JESUS' INSTRUCTIONS ON HOW AND WHAT TO PRAY. TODAY, WE PICK UP THE IDEA OF FORGIVENESS AND HOW IMPORTANT IT IS THAT WE UNDERSTAND IT. Here Paul is outlining how the knowledge of our new life should affect the way we live: how we respond to situations and interact with others.

We all have faults and it's probably easier to see them in other people than in ourselves. But just think how long it took you to learn to ride a bike, drive a car or speak another language. It took time, it took patience and it took others investing in you. Just the same applies to working out our new life. It takes time to change – and, believe it or not, others might need to forgive you because of something you've possibly said or done!

WHAT'S IT TO ME?

In my youth group, I used to pick on a guy because he annoyed me and I could easily make jokes at his expense. When I started to take my new life as a Christian seriously, I had to stop doing this and say sorry. Very graciously, he accepted my apology – but he could easily have told me to take a running jump!

THINK

Do you realise how much you have been forgiven? Do you think you're not actually that bad, and that others need much more forgiveness than you? Remember, each of us was separated from God and nothing we could do was enough to bring us back to our original relationship with Him – the friendship He intended. We make mistakes every day for which we need to say sorry to God. He is always willing to forgive us, and we need to have the same attitude, forgiving others as we have been forgiven. Remember – we sometimes need to say sorry to others as well as to God!

Do you need to take your new life in Jesus seriously and say sorry to someone?

How do we connect everything
together and live accordingly?
How do we know what is right?
How do we learn to act and react well
to what happens?

LIVING

KEY VERSE v15

'... if someone asks about your Christian hope, always be ready to explain it.'

WHY BELIEVE? WHAT WOULD IT TAKE FOR SOME OF YOUR FRIENDS TO BELIEVE IN JESUS?

I have often been in heated discussions with people about Jesus being the Son of God, about Him being an historical figure, about Him doing miracles. Yet nothing I said would convince them – even historical facts. They still wanted to see Him as, at most, a nice guy who did some nice things. Many people around at the time of Jesus had seen Him do miracles, show real intelligence in His answers, and meet their practical needs. Yet still some questioned who He was.

St Francis of Assisi said, 'Proclaim the gospel at all times and, if necessary, use words.' The apostle James puts it like this: *'Suppose you see a brother or sister who has no food or clothing, and you say, "Good-bye and have a good day; stay warm and eat well" – but then you don't give that person any food or clothing. What good does that do?'* (James 2:15–16).

By our actions people will see what we are like and will ask us questions about why we do what we do. Then we need to be able to tell them.

WHAT'S IT TO ME?

I would like to set two challenges today!

ONE: Can you tell the story of why and how you became a Christian? Try telling it out loud to yourself.

TWO: Do your words match up with your actions?

THINK

In the coming notes, we will be looking at Paul's teaching in Romans 6 and what it means for our lives. It is suggested that Paul wrote to the Church in Rome as he was planning to visit them in the future and he wanted to outline basic Christian beliefs. Paul wanted the beliefs to make a difference in these Christians' daily lives, as they should to ours today.

KEY VERSE
v1

'Well then, should we keep on sinning ... ?'

DAY 21

54

THERE IS A STORY ABOUT AN AMERICAN WHO, WHILST ON HOLIDAY, HIRED A CAR TO TOUR AROUND BRITAIN. After a few hours, he brought the car back complaining that it was very slow, used up lots of fuel and that the noise of the engine was unbearably loud.

The mechanic looked at the car and could see nothing wrong, so suggested a test drive. It soon became obvious what the problem was: the American thought the car was an automatic. He was driving a manual car around in first gear! Once he realised this, he could get a lot more from the car.

We have been saved for growth. Jesus has given us so much ability and opportunity, yet we can miss out on using our full potential in living our life for Him. '... glory to God, who is able, through his mighty power at work within us, to accomplish infinitely more than we might ask or think' (Eph. 3:20). He can do more in us, if we are willing to learn and be used by Him.

WHAT'S IT TO ME?

If we know we should be different, we should be different! We should change our ways, putting Jesus first. As it says in verse 2 of our reading: 'Since we have died to sin, how can we continue to live in it?'

THINK

Even though you have become a Christian, are you going around in first gear and not putting any of Jesus' teaching into practice? Invest time in learning what the Bible has to say about things so you can understand what Paul is saying. Think about joining a Bible study group, or ask for one to be set up. Put Jesus first in your life and get the most out of it you can.

'Don't you realize that you become the slave of whatever you choose to obey?'

DAY 22

56

I ONCE WAS A MANAGER IN A CAFÉ/NIGHTCLUB THAT WAS OPEN FROM 10.00AM TO 1.00AM THE NEXT DAY, MONDAY TO SATURDAY, AND 10.00AM TO 10.30PM ON SUNDAYS. Most weeks I was putting in 90 to 100 hours at work. I had a 12-week-old son, Tom, whom I rarely saw, and a wife who, whilst supporting me in my job, was shattered, looking after Tom and doing everything else.

I felt I had to do these hours to get the job done and to get the promotions. I did get them, but I was missing out on other things. When I was off work I still had my mobile on and often popped into work to check that everything was OK.

Paul's statement in today's reading is right: we do become the slave of whatever we choose to obey. Work was ruling my life and I realised that unless I left, I could lose my family. So I handed my notice in. What do you need to do today, to show who is in control of your life?

WHAT'S IT TO ME?

We grow up being taught by our parents, our friends, our teachers, television, radio, Internet etc. There is a saying that 'every day is a school day', meaning that every day of our lives we have the potential to learn something new. The trick is how we use the new knowledge we gain. Does it affect our lives and do we share it?

Paul believed that choosing to obey God's teaching is something to shout about and that if you take these teachings to heart, they will affect your actions.

CHALLENGE

I am still a bit of a workaholic, but obeying God and honouring my family is what I chose. How about you? Take time now to list everything you do. Are you doing anything that is not in line with what you understand God wants for your life? If you don't know how to answer this, ask a trusted Christian leader to challenge you about what they think you need to consider.

★ ★ ★ ★ ★

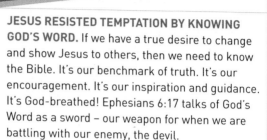

'All Scripture is inspired by God and is useful to teach us what is true and ... realize what is wrong in our lives.'

KEY VERSE v16

DAY 23

58

JESUS RESISTED TEMPTATION BY KNOWING GOD'S WORD. If we have a true desire to change and show Jesus to others, then we need to know the Bible. It's our benchmark of truth. It's our encouragement. It's our inspiration and guidance. It's God-breathed! Ephesians 6:17 talks of God's Word as a sword – our weapon for when we are battling with our enemy, the devil.

Because it is inspired by God and trustworthy, we should *read it* and *apply it* to our lives. The Bible is our standard for testing everything else that claims to be true. It is our safeguard against false teaching and our source of guidance for how we should live. It is our only source of knowledge about how we can be saved from the consequences of our sin.

God wants to show you what is true and equip you to live for Him! Have you ever spent time in God's Word? Read it regularly to discover God's truth, and to become confident in your life and faith. Develop a plan for reading the whole Bible, not just the familiar passages.

WHAT'S IT TO ME?

Read the Bible as: 'It corrects us when we are wrong and teaches us to do what is right. God uses it to prepare and equip his people to do every good work' (vv.16–17). Use its teachings to guide your conduct, so that you can make godly decisions when you're under pressure or anxious. And I hope this book helps you begin to do that.

PRAY

Father, thank You for Your Word. Thank You for inspiring others to write down Your thoughts. Help me to engage with what is in Your Word and to start to live it. Challenge me to check and test my thoughts and others' teachings against Your Word so I can have full confidence in Your leading. Amen.

'For the wages of sin is death, but the free gift of God is eternal life through Christ Jesus ...'

DAY 24

60

TODAY WE ARE TURNING ONCE AGAIN TO ROMANS CHAPTER 6. THIS CHAPTER ENDS WITH THE TWO POSSIBLE OUTCOMES FROM THE CHOICES WE MAKE – DEATH OR ETERNAL LIFE. This whole idea can be really difficult for us to understand in the world we live in.

'What, we only get *two* choices?'

In everyday life, we have loads of options available to us, from the TV channel we watch, to the flavour of crisps we eat. From what football team we choose to support, to what music we want to listen to. Every day we are faced with lots of choices, whether we notice we are making them or not. But when it comes to whom we serve, things are different. The Bible only points out a choice of two ways to go in life.

It is worth considering Newton's third law of motion: 'For every action there is an equal and opposite reaction'. The choices we make have consequences, and what we choose to do has an effect.

WHAT'S IT TO ME?

If you have asked Jesus into your life, believe He is who He said He is, and have committed your life to Him, you are in the service of God. The result of serving sin is death, but the result of serving God is life. God's life can be at work in us, transforming us: 'Now you do those things that lead to holiness ...' (v.22)

CHALLENGE

You have made that choice to follow and serve God. But are you different from when you first made your commitment to live for Him? Think of ways you feel you've changed – and any areas where there is no difference. Ask a trusted Christian leader or friend if they agree with what you think. How can you begin to work on the areas that have not changed? Reading and living out Romans 6 is a start!

'He saved us, not because of the righteous things we had done, but because of his mercy.'

THE APOSTLE PAUL IS WRITING TO TITUS, WHO WAS IN CRETE AT THE TIME, TO ENCOURAGE HIM TO CONTINUE WORKING WITH THE PEOPLE THERE, EVEN THOUGH IT WAS HARD AND THEY WERE MESSING HIM AROUND. Paul gave him some practical tips about how he could help the Cretans to overcome their past way of life and launch out into living brand-new Christian lives. And we can see that what Paul told Titus is also really relevant for us.

Have you ever made a mistake? Ever done some really good things for others? Well, God loves you, no matter how many mistakes you have made or how many good deeds you have done, or any combination of the two. He doesn't accept us because of the good stuff we do or don't do. He accepts us because He loves us. He has saved us from the mess of our old life. He has made us clean through Jesus and ready for our new life.

Over the next few days, we will be looking more at living this new life through Jesus – how it works and what it means for us today.

WHAT'S IT TO ME?

'He washed away our sins, giving us a new birth and new life through the Holy Spirit. He generously poured out the Spirit upon us through Jesus Christ ... Because of his grace he declared us righteous and gave us confidence that we will inherit eternal life' (vv.5–7).

God has declared you not guilty. You are clean before Him, not because of what you have done, but because of what Jesus has done for you! Why is this possible? Because God loves you.

PRAY

Father, thank You so much for all You have done for me; for saving me, for showing such kindness and for giving me eternal life. Help me to come to You daily to ask for forgiveness as I try to live for You. Thank You that You will always forgive me. Amen.

KEY VERSE
v13

'And don't let us yield to temptation, but rescue us from the evil one.'

DAY 26

64

THIS VERSE COMES AT THE END OF THE LORD'S PRAYER. JESUS IS TEACHING US HOW TO PRAY, SINCERELY AND HONESTLY.

In our new Christian life, we will find there are temptations from our old life. These will try to draw us back to what we used to do or the way we used to think. We need to realise that just because we have started this new life, it doesn't mean we won't get tempted to look at something we shouldn't or say something we will regret later.

Even Jesus was tempted. 'He was led by the Spirit in the wilderness, where he was tempted by the devil for forty days' (Luke 4:1–2). Who is the devil? He was once an angel called Lucifer, who decided to lead a rebellion against God. Consequently, he was thrown out of heaven with the other angels that joined him. At this point he got a name-change to Satan, or the devil.

WHAT'S IT TO ME?

The devil knew that Jesus was hungry and so tempted Him with bread. He then went on to tempt and challenge Jesus in areas where he thought He would be weak. Jesus stood up to the temptation by quoting Scripture. He came up with a system and He relied on God to get Him through.

THINK

We need to set up early warning systems to alert us to temptation. If you can identify what you are likely to be tempted by, and ask for God's help, you can find practical ways to escape the temptation. Remember to pray when you are tempted. God knows what is going on – you can't hide it. It is better to ask for help than to try to get away with doing wrong. If you do mess up, be willing to say sorry to God and ask for forgiveness. Try the Jesus prayer: 'Lord Jesus Christ, Son of God, have mercy on me, a sinner.' Repeat those words over and over as you receive His forgiveness. And read 1 John 1:8–10. He is always willing to forgive.

> 'I am the resurrection and the life. Anyone who believes in me will live, even after dying.'

KEY VERSE
V25

DAY 27

66

JESUS' CONVERSATION WITH MARTHA IN OUR READING TODAY HAPPENED IN BETWEEN LAZARUS (MARTHA'S BROTHER) DYING, AND JESUS RAISING HIM FROM THE DEAD. Martha knew who Jesus was: 'I have always believed you are Messiah, the Son of God, the one who has come into the world from God' (v.27). However, she was angry with Jesus for allowing Lazarus to die: '... if only you had been here, my brother would not have died' (v.21).

To put things into context: Martha had seen Jesus do great things and was probably asking: 'Why not me? Jesus sorts out everyone else's problems, but not mine!'

But Jesus uses the situation to explain that He is not just on earth to save Lazarus from death, but to offer eternal life to all who believe in Him (v.25). He then goes on to prove He has power over death by calling Martha's brother out of his tomb. Lazarus was raised from the dead!

★ ★ ★ ★ ★ ★ ★ ★

WHAT'S IT TO ME?

Martha knew who Jesus was and was confident about what He could do. But when He didn't turn up, and her brother died, she was understandably angry and upset.

Things don't always go the way we want them to. And sometimes, when we pray, our prayers don't seem to get answered. Or at least, they are not answered in the way we had hoped. At these times, we have to trust in God's greater plan and know that He has promised to work out all things for the good of those who love Him (see Rom. 8:28).

PRAY

Father, thank You that You know me and have a relationship with me. Thank You that I can talk to You and You listen. Thank You that I can bring everything to You. Help me to talk about my understanding of You and my frustrations with life. Challenge me to hear, and help me to learn what You say in return. Amen.

KEY VERSE v42

'My Father! If this cup cannot be taken away unless I drink it, your will be done.'

DAY 28

68

IT IS IMPORTANT TO UNDERSTAND THAT JESUS HAD A CHOICE. AT ANY POINT, HE COULD HAVE PULLED OUT OF DOING WHAT GOD HAD SENT HIM TO DO.

Instead, He sacrificed Himself so that we could have a relationship with God. He *chose* to die so that God's will could be done. He accepted the challenge of being totally separated from God, which happened when He took all the blame for our sins. He picked up the cup that was offered, and because of His obedience, we can get right with God and become everything we should be: '... to all who believed him and accepted him, he gave the right to become children of God' (John 1:12).

But He would not leave us to live for Him in our own strength. He would send His Holy Spirit to be with us always, as a comforter and encourager.

WHAT'S IT TO ME?

Are you thankful for what Jesus has done for you? If so, how do you think you should respond to Him? David, the psalmist, had this idea: 'Come, let us worship and bow down. Let us kneel before the LORD our maker, for he is our God. We are the people he watches over, the flock under his care' (Psa. 95:6–7). David suggested that we should worship God even through difficult times. God is our Creator and looks after us. He is always worthy of worship. Why not try to write your own psalm of praise to God, for who He is and what He has done for you?

PRAY

Father, help me to be willing to thank You even in the tough times. Help me to think about who You are and what You have done, and to know that You are always worthy to be praised. Thank You for all that You have done for me through Jesus. Amen.

KEY VERSES vv8–9

'For it is by grace you have been saved, through faith ... the gift of God – not by works, so that no-one can boast.' (NIV)

DAY 29

70

The hymn (church song) 'Amazing Grace' was written by John Newton around 1765. You may know the song through the film of the same name. Have a look at the words. Even though it was written over 240 years ago, the human heart stays the same.

Amazing grace! how sweet the sound
That saved a wretch like me;
I once was lost, but now am found,
Was blind, but now I see.

'Twas grace that taught my heart to fear,
And grace my fears relieved;
How precious did that grace appear,
The hour I first believed!

Through many dangers, toils and snares,
I have already come;
'Tis grace has brought me safe thus far,
And grace will lead me home.

The Lord has promised good to me,
His word my hope secures;
He will my shield and portion be,
As long as life endures.

Yes, when this flesh and heart shall fail,
And mortal life shall cease,
I shall possess, within the veil,
A life of joy and peace.

When we've been there ten thousand years,
Bright shining as the sun,
We've no less days to sing God's praise
Than when we first begun.

John Newton (1725–1807)

WHAT'S IT TO ME?

We might be used to thinking about the word 'Grace' as something religious people say at meal-times. The above hymn shows us another meaning. God's grace means this: His free, unearned favour. When we know we are accepted by God through His grace, His loving-kindness, we can relax in His unconditional love.

THINK

Do you recognise the grace you have received? Reread the Amazing Grace lyrics and quietly think about how they apply to you. Spend some time talking to God about what you have read, and thank Him for His free favour to you. As you begin to relax in His unconditional love, how might this affect others around you?

THINK ABOUT ALL THE PEOPLE YOU COME INTO CONTACT WITH. WHAT IS YOUR EFFECT ON THEM? HOW DO WE INTERACT WITH OUR FRIENDS, FAMILY ETC, AND WHAT WOULD GOD EXPECT?

OTHERS

SECTION 04//OTHERS

'Can we boast, then ... ? No, because our acquittal is not based on obeying the law [good deeds]. It is based on faith.'

DAY 30

74

TO KNOW THE WAY TO GOD, WE NEED TO KNOW JESUS. To know Jesus, we have to believe what God has said in the Bible – that we are guilty of wrong thoughts and actions and so have separated ourselves from Him. We have to be sorry for the sin in our lives, and want to change. But we also have to know that we can't get ourselves right with God. We cannot pay the price for our own sin. It's not about how good we are, how much money we give to charity, whether we work on Sundays or if we attend lots and lots of church services. We are accepted by God only through our faith in Jesus and what He has done on the cross, paying the price for our sin. To those who believe, God gives the gift of the Holy Spirit, so that we might have the power to live for Him.

WHAT'S IT TO ME?

None of us can boast that we are better in God's sight than another. We are all the same, loved and cared for. In 1 Corinthians 12:12–31, Paul explains the importance of the role each of us plays in being part of Christ's Body on earth. He shows that we all have a part to play, and even though we are all different, our part is necessary for His Body (the Church) to work. 'Yes, there are many parts, but only one body. The eye can never say to the hand, "I don't need you." The head can't say to the feet, "I don't need you"' (1 Cor. 12:20–21).

PRAY

Lord, help me to grow in my faith. Help me to be more sure of what I believe so that I experience real confidence as I talk to others about You. Help me to realise that You have given me gifts and that I should use them as part of Your Body in service to You. And thank You for encouraging me to know that I have a part to play. Amen.

'Now faith is being sure of what we hope for and certain of what we do not see.' (NIV)

DAY 31

76

YESTERDAY WE LOOKED AT THE IMPORTANCE OF FAITH. BUT WHAT *IS* FAITH? The New Living Translation tells us it 'is the confidence that what we hope for will actually happen; it gives us assurance about things we cannot see' (v.1).

In the verses that follow, we are given examples from the Bible of people that showed great faith, including Noah, who built a big boat (ark) inland, to save the animals and his family, and Abraham, who left home to follow God's instructions, although he didn't know where he would end up (Gen. 12).

Faith starts small and grows. We need to be willing to try things, and gradually our faith will develop and deepen. If you look at the characters above, you can see that God was at work in them and they knew they could trust Him. They didn't always have the answers or see the solutions, but they had an experience of God that supported and challenged them to take another step. They didn't need to see the short-term end; they were focusing on the long-term. When I say long-term, I mean an eternity spent with God. They were certain of this future without seeing it.

WHAT'S IT TO ME?

I would encourage you to find a Christian leader – someone you identify with and get along with – and ask them to become your Faith Leader for the next twelve months. Explain that you would like to be able to chat to them about faith and actions, and that you would like them to help you grow in faith over the next year. If you can, set up a meeting once a month and allow them to ask you some questions about what is going on in your life.

PRAY

Father, thank You for the faithful example that others have set. May I be an example, too. Help me to gain confidence in the future You have for me, so that I can have faith in the things I cannot yet see. Amen.

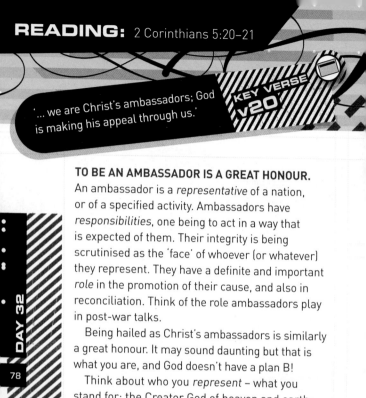

'... we are Christ's ambassadors; God is making his appeal through us.'

DAY 32

78

TO BE AN AMBASSADOR IS A GREAT HONOUR.
An ambassador is a *representative* of a nation, or of a specified activity. Ambassadors have *responsibilities*, one being to act in a way that is expected of them. Their integrity is being scrutinised as the 'face' of whoever (or whatever) they represent. They have a definite and important *role* in the promotion of their cause, and also in reconciliation. Think of the role ambassadors play in post-war talks.

Being hailed as Christ's ambassadors is similarly a great honour. It may sound daunting but that is what you are, and God doesn't have a plan B!

Think about who you *represent* – what you stand for: the Creator God of heaven and earth; the Saviour of humankind, Jesus Christ, the Lord of all. Even the wind and waves obey Him (see Matt. 8:27). There is healing in His name, cleansing power in His blood shed for us on the cross, and at the name of Jesus every knee will bow (Phil. 2:10). That is some CV!

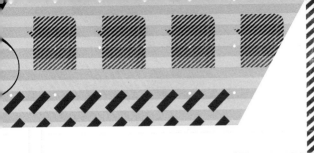

What are your *responsibilities*? Standing firm in your faith and beliefs. Having integrity in your language, attitude and lifestyle. Displaying a character that honours God.

WHAT'S IT TO ME?

What is your role? To take the message, and live out the message. To be a servant of God, for the local church and your youth group – the others need you and your gifts! You are to promote the One you represent; you're like a shop window for the kingdom of God. And you should point people towards reconciliation with the God you have come to know and follow. As Micah 6:8 says: '... do what is right ... love mercy, and ... walk humbly with your God.'

CHALLENGE

Don't live your Christian life trying to get away with as much as possible. Try to be as pure and holy as possible! Holy people are powerful people.

KEY VERSE v20

'I am praying not only for these disciples but also for all who will ever believe in me through their message.'

ONE OF THE REASONS WE KNOW JESUS IS BECAUSE OTHERS HAVE TOLD US ABOUT HIM THROUGH THEIR 'TESTIMONY' – THE STORY OF HOW THEY MET HIM. In the reading today, Jesus is praying for all the people who are going to believe in Him because of what the disciples say.

This means two things. One: Jesus is praying directly for you. Over 2,000 years ago, He was praying for you! Two: He is praying for all those people you talk to and who come to know Him because of *your* story.

In Matthew 28:18–20 Jesus gives His disciples a 'great commission': '... go and make disciples of all the nations'. We have a challenge to pass the knowledge on to our friends, family and those around us. It can sound really hard, but really it's about sharing the story of our life and faith.

DAY 33

WHAT'S IT TO ME?

Do you know your story? How is your story of knowing Jesus developing? If God has been revealed to you by Jesus, what are you going to do about it? John 17 ends with a promise, 'I have revealed you ... and I will continue to do so' (v.26). We know that this prayer is not just for the disciples back then. It's for us, too. Jesus has promised to keep revealing more and more of God to us. Could you explain why you became a Christian, in a simple way? Remember that Jesus is praying for those that come to know Him through your story. This implies that He is expecting you to share that story with others!

CHALLENGE

Think about all the things you have read in the Bible and Mettle over the last few weeks. As you reflect on what you have learned, remember: Jesus has made a way for you to be friends with God; He has all authority in heaven and on earth; He knows you individually; He cares about you; He is praying for you; and He sends you 'into the world' (v.18).

'Now I say to you that you are
Peter (which means "rock"), and
upon this rock I will build my
church, and all the powers of hell
will not conquer it.'

KEY VERSE
v18

DAY 34

82

Today and tomorrow we will be looking at what
the Bible says the Church is and should be like.
What are your thoughts on church? Is it the kind
of place where you want to spend time, or would
you never want to be seen there?

In today's reading, we can see that Jesus is
telling one of His disciples, Peter, that the Church
belongs to Him (Jesus). The Church needs to be
built on a strong foundation; this foundation is
the people who follow God – not just Peter, but
anyone who believes. Not only does Jesus tell
us of the Church's need for a strong foundation,
He also tells us that nothing, not even death and
destruction, will defeat it. Remembering this
promise from Jesus is really important in a world
where we are told that the Church is not relevant
and that it is dying.

When Jesus talks about 'church' here, He is not
talking about the building, the steeple, the bells

or the pews. He is talking about those who make up the Church. As a body of people, we belong to God and He isn't going to let our relationship with Him, or our worship, be destroyed.

WHAT'S IT TO ME?

Church is there as a help to us and to others. It is about belonging and relationship. Think about your views on church; examine your feelings. Are you going to believe what society and the world tells you, or are you going to discover for yourself the point and purpose the Church has in your friendship with God?

PRAY

Father, thank You that I am part of Your Church. Please show me more clearly how it can help me in my relationship with You. Help me to become a committed part of it too. Thank You, Lord. Amen.

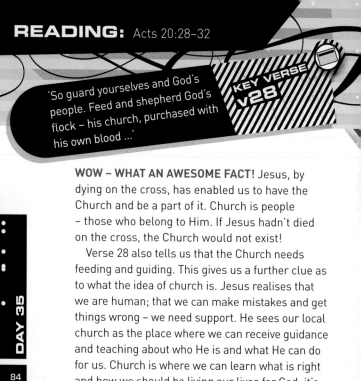

KEY VERSE v28

'So guard yourselves and God's people. Feed and shepherd God's flock – his church, purchased with his own blood ...'

WOW – WHAT AN AWESOME FACT! Jesus, by dying on the cross, has enabled us to have the Church and be a part of it. Church is people – those who belong to Him. If Jesus hadn't died on the cross, the Church would not exist!

Verse 28 also tells us that the Church needs feeding and guiding. This gives us a further clue as to what the idea of church is. Jesus realises that we are human; that we can make mistakes and get things wrong – we need support. He sees our local church as the place where we can receive guidance and teaching about who He is and what He can do for us. Church is where we can learn what is right and how we should be living our lives for God; it's the place where we can be directed by His Spirit, through the help of others.

Church leaders should also 'shepherd God's flock' – take care of church members. God's Holy Spirit has appointed them to help and lead the Church.

DAY 35

84

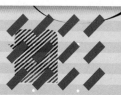

WHAT'S IT TO ME?

Have you ever seen church as being somewhere where you can learn more about God and receive guidance in how to live? A place where you can grow in your faith and be looked after; where even if you do things wrong you can go back and receive love and support? Are you willing to be part of a church?

THINK

Think about your church, or a church you could go to. Can you get involved with something that is happening there? Ask around, be willing to volunteer or say yes to helping out. Why not give up a Saturday to support an event or a weekday evening to attend a group?

Remember, you are part of the Body of Christ – His Church! So why not be an active part?

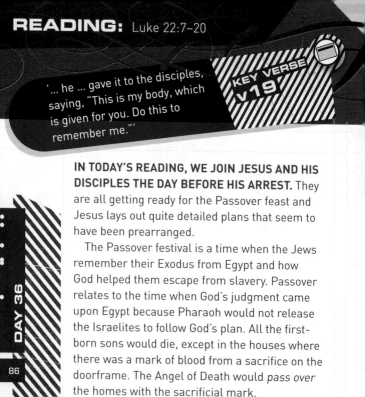

'... he ... gave it to the disciples, saying, "This is my body, which is given for you. Do this to remember me."'

KEY VERSE v19

IN TODAY'S READING, WE JOIN JESUS AND HIS DISCIPLES THE DAY BEFORE HIS ARREST. They are all getting ready for the Passover feast and Jesus lays out quite detailed plans that seem to have been prearranged.

The Passover festival is a time when the Jews remember their Exodus from Egypt and how God helped them escape from slavery. Passover relates to the time when God's judgment came upon Egypt because Pharaoh would not release the Israelites to follow God's plan. All the first-born sons would die, except in the houses where there was a mark of blood from a sacrifice on the doorframe. The Angel of Death would *pass over* the homes with the sacrificial mark.

As Jews, the disciples would have grown up participating in the Passover meal. But here, Jesus says this is the last time He will share it with them. He knew what was about to happen to Him, and the significance of the moment. Jesus was about to be the ultimate sacrifice for the whole of humankind, so that God's judgment would *pass over* those who accept Him.

WHAT'S IT TO ME?

As Jesus breaks the bread, He is showing that His body will literally be broken on the cross during the crucifixion. He then uses wine to represent His blood which would be shed for us. We are asked to continue to reflect on this moment as an act of remembering what Jesus has done in becoming the sacrifice for us all. In church, this can be part of our coming together to share communion (eating bread and drinking wine) with each other.

THINK

'This cup is the new covenant between God and his people – an agreement confirmed with my blood, which is poured out as a sacrifice for you' (v.20). God has made a promise (covenant) with all who choose to believe in Him. Make sure you remember Jesus this way whenever you can.

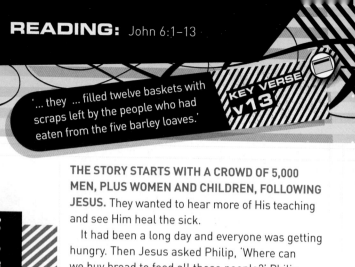

KEY VERSE
v 13

'... they ... filled twelve baskets with scraps left by the people who had eaten from the five barley loaves.'

THE STORY STARTS WITH A CROWD OF 5,000 MEN, PLUS WOMEN AND CHILDREN, FOLLOWING JESUS. They wanted to hear more of His teaching and see Him heal the sick.

It had been a long day and everyone was getting hungry. Then Jesus asked Philip, 'Where can we buy bread to feed all these people?' Philip answered, 'Even if we worked for months, we wouldn't have enough money to feed them!' Then Andrew said, 'There's a young boy here with five barley loaves and two fish. But what good is that with this huge crowd?' (see vv.5–9).

God likes to bless His people. Although following God's will won't always equal financial gain, living His way will bring 'riches' in some form. There's nothing wrong with being happy and having success – it just may not come in the way we expect it.

Always remember that it is what you do with what you've been given that really shows whether you're doing God's will. The young boy gave

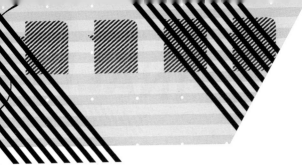

up his lunch for Jesus – a small offering – but Jesus took it and multiplied it. God gives us gifts, whether natural or material, to use for *His* purposes.

WHAT'S IT TO ME?

You may feel you haven't got much to offer but, as this story shows, a little can go a long way. The boy gave up a packed lunch and Jesus fed over 5,000 people with it.

What are you doing with the gifts God has given you? Are you storing them up or sharing them out for the benefit of others?

PRAY

Father, thank You that You have given me enough so I can share out what I have. Help me to understand that, even if I feel it isn't much, You can do great things if I am willing to offer it to You to use for Your glory. Amen.

AND FINALLY .

'God is working in you, giving you the desire and the power to do what pleases him.'

KEY VERSE v13

AS WE COME TO THE END OF THIS BOOK, LET'S HAVE A QUICK LOOK AT SOME REMINDERS AND LESSONS FROM PAUL.

Be the person God wants you to be! Take up the challenge.

God is working in you. But are you letting Him do what He wants in your life or are you fighting to do things your own way?

God is giving you the desire to obey Him. Are you listening when you feel you should talk to your non-Christian friend about church, or when you're being pressurised to drive too fast, or when you know you have had enough to drink and your friends are trying to get you to drink more?

God is giving you the power to do what pleases Him. If you do listen to God and talk to that friend, or say, 'I don't want to drive that fast' or, 'No, I've had enough', God will give you the ability to respond and the power to stick to your decision.

WHAT'S IT TO ME?

Someone always seems to be telling us that serving God means following a long list of dos and don'ts. Paul's letter to the Galatians reminds us that being a Christian isn't a matter of what we do or don't do. It's about accepting what Jesus Christ did for us, and putting Him in charge of our lives. 'So I live in this earthly body by trusting in the Son of God, who loved me and gave himself for me' (Gal. 2:20).

THINK

We have covered a lot of things over the last few weeks and, hopefully, you have been challenged. But, basically, it's a simple message: If you believe in and trust Jesus, learn about Him, talk to Him and follow Him, He will live in you.

Can you make the statement, 'Jesus is in charge of me!'? Is Jesus in charge of your life? If He is, then by trusting in the Son of God, who loved you and gave Himself for you – Christ lives in you! How does this make you feel?

'… love, joy, peace, patience, kindness, goodness, faithfulness, gentleness, and self-control. …'

DAY 39

92

HOW DO YOU TELL WHAT TYPE OF TREE YOU ARE LOOKING AT? ONE WAY IS BY ITS FRUIT. AN APPLE TREE DOES NOT PRODUCE BANANAS! This is exactly the same in our lives – how we live and act is a reflection of what we are connected to.

God sent a helper and encourager to develop 'fruit' in us. One of the fruit of the Holy Spirit is kindness. My car once broke down on the middle of a roundabout. Traffic was building up and people were beeping their horns. I got out and tried to push it to one side – quite a task when you are by yourself! Someone got out of their car, helped me and gave me a lift home. That was nine years ago and I still remember their kindness. I'm sure you can think of examples of love, patience, goodness and gentleness in your own life. Powerful fruit!

WHAT'S IT TO ME?

We have one day left and I would ask you to spend some time now considering what is going on in your life. Are there challenges you said you would do and haven't, or ones you tried but failed at. Do you need to try them again? Do you still struggle in the same areas as you did at the start of this book? Do you need to change your surroundings or the parties you go to? What will you be remembered for? What fruit do you show? Are you allowing the Holy Spirit to have a say in your life?

Remember, what we are connected to will have an affect on what we do, how we act, what we produce. Are you connected to the Spirit?

PRAY

Father, thank You that by living for You we produce such good fruit. Thank You, too, that You sent Your Holy Spirit to help us in all situations. Challenge me not become conceited or jealous of others. Help me to live by Your Spirit. Let me follow the Spirit's leading in every part of my life. Amen.

'... looking forward to what lies ahead, I press on to reach the end of the race and receive the ... prize ...'

KEY VERSES vv 13-14

DAY 40

94

I WAS SIX YEARS OLD AND AT A SCHOOL SPORTS DAY. I HAD ENTERED THE 100M RACE. We were all lined up ready to go, the pistol was fired, and we were off! I burst into the lead, running with all my heart. The finish line was ahead of me, but I wanted to see how I was doing ... so I looked back. In fact, I didn't have *that* much of a lead and in a split second I'd been overtaken. I came in third. I had lost concentration; I'd become more interested in what was going on around me, and what others were doing, and had missed out on the main prize.

What makes you turn round to see what is happening? What causes you to become distracted? Paul says in his letter that he has not reached perfection, but he *does* know what the prize will be and he wants to push on towards it. These are not just words. Paul has been in prison, been beaten, been chased out of towns and now faces execution – all for what he believes.

WHAT'S IT TO ME?

So what was Paul's secret of total focus on the finish line and the prize? Simply this: 'Don't worry about anything; instead, pray about everything. Tell God what you need, and thank him for all he has done. Then you will experience God's peace, which exceeds anything we can understand. His peace will guard your hearts and minds as you live in Christ Jesus' (Phil. 4:6–7).

Paul is encouraging us to look ahead; to press on to reach the end of the race (our lives) and receive the prize – eternal life with God.

PRAY

Father, thank You for Paul's advice and encouragement. Thank You that I can bring everything that troubles me to You. Remind me of this if I start to stress and get uptight, angry, worried or afraid. Help me not to get bogged down with things that distract me from finishing the race. And challenge me to live all-out for You! Amen.

OUTRO

As we come to the end of our exploration of the basics of faith, let us encourage you to try to create a habit of reading your Bible and spending time every day with God. Look back at what you signed up to when you started this book. Can you continue, or do you need to do it differently?

If you connected with these notes we also produce daily notes that come out every four months: *Mettle* Bible reading notes. These will help you understand more of God's Word and find ways to apply what you have learned to your everyday life.

Remember, things change but God remains the same – Hebrews 13:8. So, whatever is happening (or has yet to happen) in your life, God will be there for you. With the help of the Bible, God's Holy Spirit and other Christians you can learn how to cope, day to day, and prepare for your future with God at the centre.

Keep going and be assured of our prayers as you continue on your journey of faith!

The *Mettle* team